SO – YOU'RE A CHRISTIAN POLITICIAN?

Narrated by

CARL ARMSTRONG

Cover Photo

Don Durbridge, Media Host and Interviewer.[1]

i

So ~ You're a Christian Politician?
Copyright © 2014 Carl Armstrong. All rights reserved.

Published by: Silver DaySpring Publishing

The Lord gave the word and great was the company of those who published it." (Psalms 68:11)

ISBN: 978-1495288760
ISBN-13: 1495288765

iii

ACKNOWLEDGEMENT

Who am I, how did I get here and what is my relationship to the Divine, to nations and to society in general? Mankind has struggled with these questions from time immemorial.

This book of less than one hundred pages is presented as a 'Reader's Digest' condensation of salient points and themes from a much larger book entitled *Waters of Creativity*—a docudrama[2] of twelve presidential style debates between secular scientists and theologians with scientific credentials.

Bible Quotes are from the American King James Bible unless otherwise stated[3] (Bolding of selected phrases has been added by the author for emphasis of themes).

INTRODUCTION

Born in Cherokee, Oklahoma, Roger Wilson Smith rose through the political ranks to become governor of Oklahoma. This is the story of his journey to become United States presidential candidate Smith in the 2020 election. Has he been elected?—that is the unfinished part of this story.

However, when it comes to aspiring presidential candidates, one of the press' favorite games is the hope of getting a 'gotcha' comment that will lead to increased ratings for their media outlet. So, whether the personal beliefs of the person doing the interview is left, or right or in between—the interview is often a cat and mouse game between interviewer and the candidate.

In the intense spotlight of today's electronic media, one off the cuff remark can dog the candidate and become the fodder for oft repeated political ads. So often, the brief video excerpts are excised in such a way that distorts the candidate's true beliefs.

However—on the positive side—a proverb states *A word fitly spoken is like apples of gold in pictures of silver*   (Proverbs 25:11).

A presidential candidate deals with a wide range of inquiries. This book chronicles only those snippets of questions and replies **specifically related** to Governor Smith's Christian beliefs—from his announcement as a presidential candidate to the month of the Hashtag Party National Convention.

The media has often questioned a statement made by then candidate Smith in the 2016 gubernatorial debates. He said, "Science is only now beginning to catch up with the truths revealed in the Bible." Their observation was that it may play well in Muskogee, but will it play in New York?

CONTENTS

DEDICATION

to Jesus of Nazareth

Without the ministry of Jesus Christ, there would be no Christian religion. Christian politicians would not exist or be questioned about their beliefs.

Jesus often taught by answering a question with a question or by making a statement that prompted an action. Here are three examples from scripture:

- And he said unto them, Whose is this image and superscription?
- They say to him, Caesar's. Then said he to them, Render therefore unto Caesar the things which are Caesar's; and unto God the things that are God's.
- When they had heard these words, they marveled, and left him, and went their way. (Matthew 22:20-22)

- So when they continued asking him, he lifted up himself, and said unto them, He that is without sin among you, let him first cast a stone at her. (John 8:7)

- And when he was come into the temple, the chief priests and the elders of the people came unto him as he was teaching, and said, By what authority do you do these things? and who gave you this authority?

- The baptism of John, from where was it? from heaven, or of men? And they reasoned with themselves, saying, If we shall say, From heaven; he will say unto us, Why did ye not then believe him?
- But if we shall say, Of men; we fear the people; for all hold John as a prophet.
- And they answered Jesus, and said, We cannot tell. And he said unto them, Neither tell I you by what authority I do these things. (Matthew 21:24-27)

A question is often cloaked with an outward wrapping that springs from an inner motive. Jesus knew what was in men's hearts and answered in a way that revealed the inner motive.

The scriptures tell us *the word of God is quick, and powerful, and sharper than any two edged sword, piercing even to the dividing asunder of soul and spirit, and of the joints and marrow, and is a **discerner of the thoughts and intents of the heart**.*

(Hebrews 4:12)

1 ONWARD AND UPWARD!

Stillwater, Oklahoma, October 1, 2019:

After months of speculation—and several visits to Iowa and New Hampshire—Governor Roger Smith chose the Oklahoma State University Aviation and Space campus to make his formal announcement for a presidential bid. He laid out his plans for moving the economy onward past its malaise and providing leadership to uplift the morale of America toward a brighter future. …

Reporter: Governor Smith, I can understand that you chose this campus for your announcement because of its forward looking space program. However, you profess to be a devout Christian—how do you reconcile the current knowledge of space with the archaic flat earth and earth centrist concepts put forth by the church in the Galileo's era? Isn't the Bible a little out of date?

RWS: That is an excellent question and I will answer it by first asking you a question. Look at the large NASA photo of the earth taken from space on the side of this assembly hall. Now, I am going to describe that photo to you and ask you a question about my description of it.

Reporter: OK, please do.

The blue marble: Courtesy NASA

RWS: The earth seems to be hanging on nothing in space. I see white clouds floating just above its surface. I see the circle of the globe as if it were marked out by a compass. I see the boundary between day and night on this beautiful blue marble. Would you say that is an apt description?

Reporter: It seems to be in order, what is your point?

RWS: Now, I'm going to read you a description from a book describing the very earliest phase of space exploration.

> - He stretches out the north over the empty place, and **hangs the earth on nothing.**
> - He binds up the waters in his thick clouds; and the cloud is not rent under them.
> - He holds back the face of his throne, and **spreads his cloud on it.**
> - He has **compassed the waters with bounds**, until the **day and night come to an end.**
>
> (JOB 26:7-10)

My question for you is to explain how this amazing description of the earth hanging in space was written in the Bible by the patriarch Job thirty-five hundred years ago? He even wrote about the earth being round (compassed) rather than being flat.

Reporter: I can't explain it—it is sort of amazing.

RWS: One can only ponder how Job obtained the information to write this description. Was he shown it in a vision or possibly somehow even experienced it? It does not seem to be within our human comprehension that he rode a rocket into orbit and observed the earth hanging in space.

Consider the jolt in perspective described by Apollo 12 astronaut Alan Bean on his launch into space and on to the moon. He made these comments about the launch and his first impressions of earth.[4]

> "The thought that ran through my head was, 'I hope the metal in this space ship is strong enough to withstand the vibration. It is more than I ever imagined that machinery could stand and still operate.
>
> *I looked for the wire that is holding this earth up for a second.* You can't suddenly change from an earthling to a spaceling.'"

Alan Bean's reaction was much like that recorded by Job when Job wrote … *hangs the earth on nothing.*

Next question to the gentleman in row 3 …

2 A WOMAN AS VICE PRESIDENT OR CHIEF JUSTICE?

Cleveland, Ohio, December 5, 2020

Governor R.W. Smith paid a visit to our city today to speak to the National Association of Professional Women's conference. After his presentation he opened up the floor for questions which were very much on the minds of professional women. …

Jane W: Governor, I am concerned about whether your Christian background and possible ideas on man/woman submission would preclude you from selecting a woman as a vice-presidential running mate. Or how about appointing a woman as Chief Justice of the Supreme Court—should an opening exist. What is your attitude about this?

RWS: Our country has many women qualified to be vice-president or president for that matter. For me, it would simply come down to picking the most qualified candidate regardless of gender. Concerning the position of Chief Justice, it would certainly be biblical to have a woman Chief Justice—there is one in the Bible.

Jane W: You're kidding—I've never heard of such a thing! I thought the male Patriarchs and Pharisees did all that.

RWS: Oh, yes—it's in the Bible, I will read it to you. I have the Bible text bookmarked on my tablet.

> • And Deborah, **a prophetess**, the wife of Lapidoth, **she judged Israel at that time**.
> • And she dwelled under the palm tree of Deborah between Ramah and Bethel in mount Ephraim: and the children of Israel came up to her for judgment (Judges 4:4-5)

So, there it is, she was the Judge or Chief Justice for all of Israel—composed of men as well as women.

And, I suppose God wanted to have her in that position because the prophet Samuel wrote in the seventh chapter, verse eleven of his second book that the Lord *commanded judges to be over my people*

Israel … And, by the way, Deborah was a very successful and competent judge.

Jane W: Interesting—were there, shall I say, other professional women described in the Bible?

RWS: Oh, yes. Huldah, resident of the Jerusalem College, was a prophetess and counselor to the king. (II Chronicles 34:22) Lydia had a professional business as a merchant of purple. (Acts 16:14) Mary Magdalene was a prophetess and close confidant of Jesus.

And, the ministry of Jesus and the disciples was very much supported by women of *substance*. To me, substance means they were very professional managers. The scripture names *Joanna the wife of Chuza Herod's steward, and Susanna, and many others, which ministered to him of their substance.* (Luke 8:3) Does that answer your question?

Jane W: Yes, it does, but not exactly the way I expected. However, my friend Patricia has some questions—she is waving to me—so I suppose she wants to ask them herself.

Patricia L: Yes, I do. What about this thing of submission of women to men? I have run across men in the past who want to put me in my place.

RWS: Well, I will admit there are different ideas on this, but there is a very simple way of explaining it. When I have asked men whether they want to be part of the *bride of Christ* at his coming, they definitely express this desire. But, then on second thought, they wonder how they can be a bride.

You see, **men** (as well as women) **conceive thoughts in their mind, brain, psyche or soul**—whatever you want to call it. **Conception is a female attribute**. Our mind can be chaste and willing to receive thoughts from God—or not so chaste and receive thoughts from an evil source. And when the seed of thoughts grow, it may bring forth good or evil depending on the source of the seed. So, **men have a feminine component in their soul.**

However, the Bible shows that both men and women have an **inner man**, which is their **human spirit**. The seed of good thoughts come from the God given inner man which should be the husband of the soul. So, true submission is not so much physical gender related—instead, **it is receiving pure thoughts through our husband** (inner man) **spirit and conceiving those thoughts in our feminine mind or soul**. In Christ, **both** men and women are called to do this regardless of the natural gender of our body.

Even Jesus, in his Garden of Gethsemane experience, had to make this choice in his **soul** and he found it to be an extremely difficult and troubling choice. He said *My **soul** is exceeding sorrowful ... the **spirit** indeed is willing, but the flesh is weak.* (Matthew Chapter 26)

Patricia L: This conceiving of thoughts thing by men as well as women sort of makes sense to me,

8

but I find your use of terms like spirit as the husband and the soul as the woman confusing—would you elaborate a bit on that?

RWS: The Apostle Paul spoke of our make-up as having three parts: spirit, soul, and body. (I Thess 5:23) The spirit seems to be located in the heart abdominal area. No doubt, you've had what is known as a 'gut feeling' about something—when at the same time— in the mind or soul, it just doesn't make logical sense. Think of one's spirit as the heart and the soul as the head. Women are much more skilled than men in being in touch intuitively with their inner man spirit.

Patricia L: I can understand that, I have had intuitive feelings about some situations and my husband has ignored them to his later regret. However, I still want to know—is your wife in submission to you?

RWS: I'm not sure how to answer. Perhaps, that is a good question for my wife.

Audience: Laughter

RWS: Let me put it this way—as my wife and I share love with each other and love our Lord, distinctions of natural gender disappear. The Apostle Paul described the desired result:

- There is neither Jew nor Greek, there is neither bond nor free, there is

neither male nor female: **for you are all one** in Christ Jesus. (Galations 3:28).

Patricia L: Thank you for your answers—I will have to think about what you said.   …

3 PIGEON DROPPINGS

Princeton, NJ, January 7, 2020

After attending a breakfast rally in Concord, New Hampshire, Governor R.W. Smith came to Princeton where he addressed a gathering of enthusiastic students. He spoke of the disillusionment in general that college graduates have had in seeking employment. However, he praised the scientific curricula at Princeton, and proposed his plan for revitalizing the horizons for science in America. Afterward, he took questions from students …

Student A: You once said that science has a lot of catching up in order to confirm the truths contained in the Bible. In my view of modern science, that brash statement seems a tall mountain for you to have to climb. Is that your belief now? If so, give us some examples of this, please.

RWS: Have you ever heard the pigeon droppings story?—a Princeton professor, Robert H. Dicke, was instrumental in solving this mystery.[5]

Student A: Not sure if I have, please go on.

RWS: It goes like this: In 1964, near Holmdel, NJ, Bell Lab scientists Arno Penzias and Robert Wilson built a horn type radio receiver to receive radio waves bounced off Echo balloon satellites. It worked to a degree but they could not eliminate a strange hissing noise which was interfering with getting a clear signal.

They checked for local electrical interference, removed leaves that drifted into the antennae, tried cooling the receiver, nothing removed the hissing. And then, a pigeon's nest and associated droppings was removed from the antennae. Still, the hissing continued and they found that no matter where the antenna was aimed in the sky, they still received the hissing signal.

Then, Princeton professor Dicke and associates learned of this mystery and were able to explain it as cosmic background radiation left-over from the big bang.

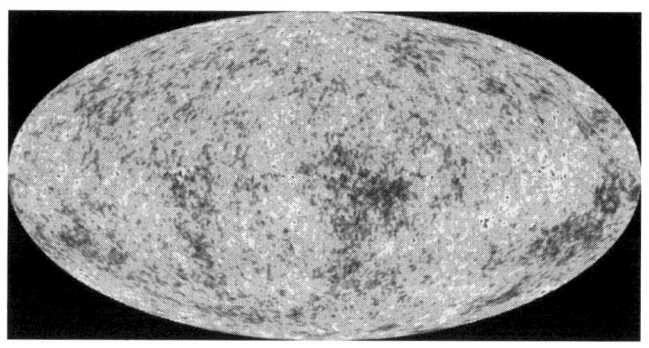

Nine Year Microwave Sky by WMAP Satellite[6]

Now, you can go online and see the picture of the infant universe that WMAP and other satellite technologies revealed. ... I have the image bookmarked on my tablet—I will hold it up so you in the back can see it

Now, you may remember that the Bell Lab researchers were absolutely amazed that they received this hissing signal from **every**—note I emphasize **every**—part of the sky, no matter where they aimed it. Now, consider this observation written in the Psalms by King David tens of centuries ago:

- The heavens declare the glory of God; and the firmament shows his handiwork.
- Day to day utters speech, and night to night shows knowledge.
- **There is no speech nor language, where their voice is not heard**.

(Psalms 19:1-3)

Don't you find it amazing—that no matter where they pointed their antenna into the sky, there is not any place *where their voice is not heard*? And, it was not until 1964 that this was understood.

Student A: That I'll have to think about …

RWS: Princeton has a Christian history. New Light Presbyterians founded the College of New Jersey, later Princeton University, in 1746 in order to train ministers.[7] Certainly one of its more famous academics was Albert Einstein. I suppose that since its all relative anyway, we can say the earth went down instead of mankind's conventional saying that the sun came up—or maybe the road crossed the chicken?

Audience: Laughter

Student A: Your example about the voice of background radiation is interesting—but we run radioactive decay profiles which seem to indicate that the earth and the universe—as illustrated by the WMAP satellite data is billions of years old. Some of my Christian friends beg to differ saying the earth and universe is only thousands of years old. Haven't you dug yourself a hole that you can't get out of?

RWS: I don't think so—let me explain it this way. The scriptures tell us Adam was created from dust. Where did that dust come from?—most likely the earth. Would you agree from your scientific investigations that the ingredients which ultimately formed the earth came from the dust in the cosmos?

Student A: That's what our professors tell us—but that dust is billions of years old—not just thousands.

RWS: Good, thank you for your observation. Now, would it surprise you to know the Bible says that before the features of the earth were brought forth, the ingredients came from *the highest part of the dust of the world.*

Student A: Yes it would, is that in the Bible?

RWS: Well, yes it is, it is recorded in the eighth chapter of the book of Proverbs which was written by King Solomon. The beginning of this chapter discusses the virtue of Wisdom which some say is the canvas on which God brings forth creation—and Wisdom was with God from the very beginning when the cosmos was just dust.

- The LORD possessed me in the beginning of his way, before his works of old.
- I was set up from everlasting, **from the beginning, or ever the earth was.**
- When there were no depths, I was brought forth; when there were no fountains abounding with water.
- Before the mountains were settled, before the hills was I brought forth:
- While as yet he had not made the earth, nor the fields, **nor the highest part of the dust of the world.** (Proverbs 8:22-26)

So, there it is, the highest part of the dust of the world. And then out of that dust the earth came forth. The scriptures even tell us that a compass (draws a circle) was set on the face of the depth (the oceans). Imagine that they knew the earth's shape was circular way back then.

- When he prepared the heavens, I was there: when **he set a compass on the face of the depth**:
- When he established the clouds above: when he strengthened the fountains of the deep:
- When he gave to the sea his decree, that the waters should not pass his commandment: **when he appointed the foundations of the earth:**

- Then I was by him, as one brought up with him: and I was daily his delight, rejoicing always before him;
. Rejoicing in the habitable part of his earth; and my delights were with the sons of men. (Proverbs 8:27-31)

In the beginning the earth (dust) was *without form*. How old was that dust that went into formation of the earth? Was it thousands of years old, millions, billions, trillions?—the Bible doesn't seem to say. Maybe, your rate of radioactive decay and calculations on the age of the cosmos is right—time will tell. But, I find it quite interesting that the theories of your professors about the accretion of the dust into galaxies, stars and planets and the ancient Bible's discussion of the *higher part of the dust of the world* seem to agree.

And also, it would seem that there was initially only *the habitable part of his earth*, maybe there was *planted a garden eastward in Eden:*

Student A: You're not telling me what I expected you to tell me—are you a young earth creationist or an old earth creationist?

RWS: Go with me on a little adventurous trip and you can decide that for yourself. Suppose a **1000 year old redwood**, as determined by **radiometric tree rings**, falls in California and no one is there to hear the sound. You and I manage to buy the dusty old lumber and take **one year** to build a house.

Does that make us a one year **young house creationist** or a 1001 year **old house creationist**? Do we date the earth's age **before it even rotates** as a ball of earth?

Student A: Well, sort of depends on **the definition of a day as a starting point**—hmmm—I'll think about it? I find all this new and quite interesting, but I wonder if you have just cherry picked a few examples that go toward proving your point.

RWS: Oh, there are many more examples that I could give where the answers that science is just now 'discovering' were written in antiquity in the Bible.

Student B: OK, you're on—give us another example.

RWS: OK, have you studied the magnetosphere which protects the earth from the bulk of the harmful solar wind radiation coming from the sun?

Student B: Yes, but is that in the Bible?

RWS: You're a perfect straight man—wait and see and then make up your own mind. The understanding of the true nature of the magnetosphere began in the 1930's and the Explorer series of missions in the 1950's greatly advanced our knowledge. But, is this shielding of the earth described in the Bible?

Artist's rendition of the magnetosphere[8] - deflecting harmful radiation from the sun past the earth

. For the LORD God is a **sun and shield**: the LORD will give grace and glory: no good thing will he withhold from them that walk uprightly. (Psalms 84:11)

Here we have the sun and shield mentioned in the same verse. What about shielding the earth?

• The princes of the people are gathered together, even the people of the God of Abraham: **for the shields of the earth belong to God**: he is greatly exalted. (Psalms 47:9)

Student B: I can kind of see how you're coming up with this, but I suppose these verses could be interpreted differently. OK, three examples, is that all you have?

RWS: Oh, not at all, I have many, many more. Hmmm … let's try this one. We'll do it a little different this time, I will give the scriptures first and then we will discuss it in terms of modern technology. The Bible mentions the term four winds numerous times, so there must be something unique about having four winds. In the interest of brevity, I will give you two scriptures about the winds.

- The wind goes toward the south, and turns about to the north; it whirls about continually, and the wind returns again according to his circuits. (Ecclesiastes 1:6)

- And he shall send his angels with a great sound of a trumpet, and they shall gather together his elect from the four winds, from one end of heaven to the other. (Matthew 24:31)

I noted that Princeton offers doctoral degrees in General Atmospheric Sciences and Meteorology. So, unless you're in that curricula, you may want to ask your professors about the diagram that I'm about to show you on my tablet.

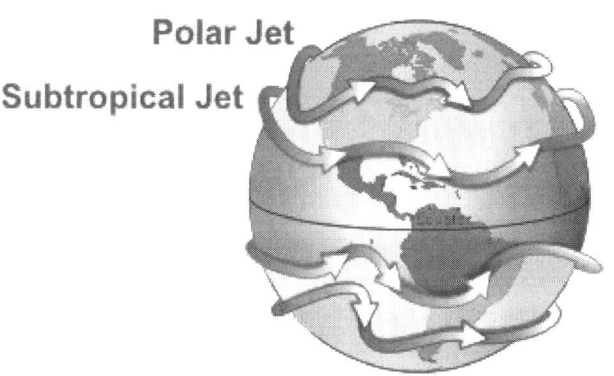

Polar Jet

Subtropical Jet

Actual jet stream configuration[9]

(National Oceanic and Atmospheric Administration)

Note that there are four jet streams that *whirl about continually* between the north and the south. I suppose it is more modern to call them jet streams instead of winds now since everyone is familiar with jet planes. Maybe the mentioning of the four winds is not that remarkable—but put together with the references to the **polar vortex** *circuits* of the jet streams; it is remarkable for the days of yore.

Do you want me to give more examples? How about all the reasons that earth is in the 'Goldilocks' zone? Everything is *just right* including distance from the sun, axial tilt, air composition for breathing, abundant water.

The earth's magnetic field shields us from intense radiation. The sun's heliosheath shields us from deadly deep space radiation. The moon stabilizes the earth's orbital axis. The gravitational field of Jupiter pulls in a major portion of asteroids that might otherwise impact the earth. Shall I go on?

Student B: No—that's not necessary—even our professors use the term 'Goldilocks' zone.   …

4 MERCY REJOICES AGAINST JUDGMENT

Houston, Texas, February 1, 2020

Presidential candidate and Governor R.W. Smith visited Houston Baptist University today for a prayer luncheon that included ministers from all across the Houston area. Each speaker was invited to speak for several minutes about one of their favorite Bible verses. Governor Smith chose James 2:13 which reads: *For he shall have judgment without mercy, that has showed no mercy; and mercy rejoices against judgment.*

He posed the question of what churches and society in general can do in the way of helping those with drug, alcohol and mental health issues—rather than judging them such that they become outcasts of society. He related the horror that he felt as a seventeen year old when apprehended and jailed for a crack cocaine drug offense. Making the phone call to tell his parents was gut wrenching, but to his immense relief, his parents and friends were supportive.

He said, "In the end, the judge was merciful—the punishment was constructive, and actually a blessing in disguise. Having a need to obtain mercy greatly facilitates understanding why mercy rejoices against judgment. Another of my favorite scriptures is *Mercy and truth are met together; righteousness and peace have kissed each other.*(Psalms 85:10)"

After the luncheon, Governor Smith paused in the parking lot before boarding the campaign bus for an impromptu session with reporters, students and some of the pastors that had attended. As might be expected, several of the questions involved social issues. …

Student: Governor Smith, I have a question about the use of executive orders. How much latitude does the president have to pick and choose what should be enforced and what can be revised or overlooked—for example retaining crack cocaine as a substance regulated under federal law?

RWS: The oath of office reads: I do solemnly swear

that I will faithfully execute the office of President of the United States, and will to the best of my ability, preserve, protect, and defend the Constitution of the United States. One of the duties of the president is to faithfully execute the laws. Congress makes the laws; the president enforces them. To the best of my ability I would do what I promised to do.

Counselor: Governor Smith, I counsel women from broken families, pregnant unwed teens and single moms on an almost daily basis. I see the anguish of young girls suddenly realizing they have a child developing inside them. Perhaps, you can—maybe, just a little bit—empathize with this from your own experience of being jailed and dreading to tell your parents. Do you have any comments on this either from a Christian standpoint or a governmental standpoint?

RWS: Yes, in my case, my view of my heavenly Father changed from someone wanting to whack me with a big stick every time I got out of line to a Father with loving arms extended welcoming his prodigal son back into the household.

From a woman's standpoint, Jesus' love and compassion extended to the woman about to be stoned when he said *He that is without sin among you, let him first cast a stone at her.* (John 8:7)

Yes, truth is truth, but truth administered with love results in mercy rejoicing against judgment.

I was fortunate in coming from a home where my parents were nurturing and accepting and were able to provide my basic needs. It seems that our government in general has overlooked root causes that stem from broken families. Tax policies and assistance policies need to be revised to provide healing of family relationships rather than promoting further fracturing.

Reporter: Governor Smith, I'm a grizzled old reporter that's been hanging around Houston for fifty years, and, as you might guess, I'm somewhat skeptical and even cynical about politicians. I like your love and mercy message, but let's get down to the real nitty-gritty.

As you know, the Texas Late Term Abortion Law has been in and out of the courts since it was passed in 2013—it deals with pregnancy termination in the third trimester. This law was passed around the time of a Philadelphia court case. A doctor was charged with removing third trimester babies from the womb and using scissors to cut the spinal cord of live, breathing babies—babies that were to that moment surviving outside the womb.

Would you please comment on the Texas law from either a political or spiritual perspective?

RWS: I find it particularly interesting, and almost ironic, that I am asked this question on the campus parking lot of Houston Baptist University. Since it is a Baptist University, I will try to answer the question from a spiritual and biblical perspective (I realize that from a political perspective, this is a hotbed of controversy affecting the lives of millions of women—and I am respectful of their concerns).

You probably well know the circumstances concerning the birth of John the Baptist—the child given to Zacharias and Elizabeth. I'll find the scriptures here on my tablet with the Bible software. When the angel told Zacharias that his barren wife would conceive a child he questioned the angel saying: *Whereby shall I know this? for I am an old man, and my wife well stricken in years.*

How old are you, Mr. Grizzled Reporter?

Reporter: I am seventy-two years old.

RWS: Imagine if you went home today and your wife said, "Dear, I have something to tell you, we have a little bundle of joy headed our way, and it's not a grandchild."

Audience: Laughter.

RWS: I won't query you on your views about abortion by potential parents in the forty to fifty year old range. However, you did ask me to comment on the Texas Late Term Abortion law, so here are my comments from a spiritual perspective.

You well know the story of how the angel appeared to Mary and the child Jesus was conceived in her womb. Here is the story:

- And the angel answered and said to her, The Holy Ghost shall come on you, and the power of the Highest shall overshadow you: therefore also that holy thing which shall be born of you shall be called the Son of God.
- And, behold, your cousin Elisabeth, she has also conceived a son in her old age: and **this is the sixth month with her, who was called barren.**
- For with God nothing shall be impossible.
- And Mary said, Behold the handmaid of the Lord; be it to me according to your word. And the angel departed from her.
- And Mary arose in those days, **and went into the hill country with haste, into a city of Juda**;
- And entered into the house of Zacharias, and saluted Elisabeth. (Luke 1:35-40)

Now, it is apparent from these scriptures that Mary wasted little time getting to Elisabeth's house about the time of Elisabeth's sixth month of pregnancy.

Let's read what happened next:

> • And it came to pass, that, when Elisabeth heard the salutation of Mary, **the babe leaped in her womb**; and Elisabeth was filled with the Holy Ghost:
> • And she spoke out with a loud voice, and said, Blessed are you among women, and blessed is the fruit of your womb.
> • And what is this to me, that the mother of my Lord should come to me?
> • For, see, as soon as the voice of your salutation sounded in my ears, **the babe leaped in my womb for joy**. (Luke 1:41-44)

Was the baby John the Baptist in Elisabeth's womb some unknowing vegetable like entity devoid of emotions such as joy or pain? Apparently not, for as Elisabeth said, *the babe leaped in my womb for joy.*

What if Zacharias and Elisabeth had become dismayed at having a pregnancy in their old age and had it terminated. Think about it.

Sir, I have this question for you: If. John the Baptist, the wee one in Elisabeth's womb, had been terminated, would we be standing here today on the campus of Houston Baptist University?

Reporter: No, we most likely would not be standing here. And other denominations with churches named after John the Baptist would not have that name. …

5 RUNNING THE RACE TO RECEIVE THE PRIZE

Daytona, Florida, February 22, 2020

Governor R.W. Smith spoke at a prayer breakfast held at the Daytona Beach Conference Center yesterday. A significant number of NASCAR drivers were there and the governor plans to attend the Daytona 500 race today. His scripture text was from I Corinthians 9:24.

> *Know you not that they which run in a race run all, but one receives the prize? So run, that you may obtain.*

… After the prayer breakfast had ended, the governor responded to questions from a large number of attendees that remained to meet with him.

Attendee A: What do you think the founding fathers

would think of government's role today?

RWS: Well, shucks, let me revert back to my good ol' days in Oklahoma at the fairs where I raced horses. A good horse race has a dozen or so entries and that's what makes it interesting. If I didn't win, I would look at what the winners were doing, make some adjustments or get a different horse and try again next year.

That strategy comes from the genius of our founders who set up thirteen different horses (states) to run the race. Yes, there would be some laggard horses along the way, but the losers could learn from the winners. And those states that let the counties and the local districts participate in the races benefit from the same strategy (ancient Israel was founded on a similar strategy of thirteen tribes).

Now, suppose the Federal government decided that there should be only one type of horse and it should be trained according to its manuals—it would be a pretty dull and unproductive horse race. I doubt there would be much interest in the Daytona 500 if the government designed two or maybe three or four clunkers to run in the race.

Let me quote just a bit from The Declaration of Independence:

> When in the Course of human events, it becomes necessary for one people to dissolve the political bands which have connected them with another,

and to assume, among the Powers of the earth, the separate and equal station to which the Laws of Nature and of Nature's God entitle them, a decent respect to the opinions of mankind requires that they should declare the causes which impel them to the separation.

We hold these truths to be self-evident, that all men are created equal, that they are endowed by their Creator with certain unalienable Rights, that among these are Life, Liberty, and the pursuit of Happiness.

Of course, we know the context of the circumstance which caused our founding fathers to seek relief from the whims and yokes of the king of England. Instead, they very wisely put themselves under their Creator which is referred to as Nature's God. But this was not the first time a nation made a choice between having a king over them—or alternately, have the Creator rule over them. I take you back to the days of Samuel the prophet who warned Israel what would happen if they had a king ruling over them. Is that situation very much different from what we see in the concentration of power in the hands of a few today?

- Then all the elders of Israel gathered themselves together, and came to Samuel to Ramah,

- And said to him, Behold, you are old, and your sons walk not in your ways: **now make us a king to judge us like all the nations.**
- But the thing displeased Samuel, when they said**, Give us a king to judge us**. And Samuel prayed to the LORD.
- And the LORD said to Samuel, **Listen to the voice of the people in all that they say to you: for they have not rejected you, but they have rejected me, that I should not reign over them.**
- According to all the works which they have done since the day that I brought them up out of Egypt even to this day, with which they have forsaken me, and served other gods, so do they also to you.
- Now therefore listen to their voice: **however, yet protest solemnly to them, and show them the manner of the king that shall reign over them.**
- And Samuel told all the words of the LORD to the people that asked of him a king.

(1 Samuel 8:4-10)

Now, one might wonder whether America is rejecting the Creator by a very targeted effort to remove any mention of Him from schools, government proceedings or even in the military. And those in the military unfortunately are quite aware of the possibility of death. There is an old saying: *There are not many atheists in foxholes.*

Do we want an all-powerful government to be king over us? Perhaps, we call our leader president, but is it progressing toward being king, emperor, czar, dear leader, or monarch? (I suppose if I'm elected, I may live to regret these words, but I would reverse the trends of past years).

Audience: Laughter

RWS: So, what was the warning that Samuel gave to the people of Israel?—we will read on.

- And he said, This will be the manner of the king that shall reign over you: **He will take your sons, and appoint them for himself, for his chariots, and to be his horsemen**; and some shall run before his chariots.
- And he will appoint him captains over thousands, and captains over fifties; and will set them to ear his ground, and to reap his harvest, **and to make his instruments of war**, and instruments of his chariots.
- And he will take **your daughters to be confectionaries, and to be cooks, and to be bakers.**
- And he will **take** your fields, and your vineyards, and your olive groves, even the best of them, and **give them to his servants.**
- And he will take the **tenth** of your seed, and of your vineyards, and give to his officers, and to his servants.

- And he will take your menservants, and your maidservants, and your best young men, and your asses, and put them to his work.
- He will take the **tenth** of your sheep: **and you shall be his servants.**
- And you shall cry out in that day because of your king which you shall have chosen you; and the LORD will not hear you in that day.

(I Samuel 8:11-18)

Gee, folks, wouldn't it be great if our taxes were only 10% of our income—who can remember days when it was that low? But, there is good news, if we set our course to pursue it.

- If my people, which are called by my name, **shall humble themselves, and pray,** and seek my face, and turn from their wicked ways; then will I hear from heaven, and will forgive their sin, and **will heal their land**.

(II Chronicles 7:14)

Perhaps that's a somewhat lengthy answer to your question, but does it suffice?

Attendee A: I think so; however I never really expected those words to come out of the mouth of a modern presidential candidate.

RWS: Next question.

Attendee B: Religious freedom—or the lack

thereof—is a hot topic these days. There are many religions in the world and even atheism which is sort of a religion in itself. Since you are a Christian, how would you handle this in the way of policy decisions?

RWS: I think in the days of the framing of the constitution, America was pretty much a Judeo-Christian nation—and the founder's main concern was this denomination or that one gaining power and forcing its doctrine upon the people. They, as shown in the Declaration of Independence, believed in Nature's God and the Creator. Also, they wanted to guard against any particular denomination being a state church.

During the last fifty years or so, America has become much more variegated in terms of peoples and religions from all over the world. Some of these religions, and even Christianity to a degree in past centuries, have tried to force their beliefs upon the people basically saying my way or the highway—or even worse.

I do believe that America is a *city set on a hill* and the light of that city is drawing many peoples to it— we are not a nation that has to build walls to keep people from escaping. That light is a freedom to worship God or even the Nogod religion of atheism.

No matter what policy is in place, it is unlikely that everyone will be satisfied. However, there is a huge, huge difference between free participation in a society and forced conversion to the majority's dogma—just ask some of the Christians being severely persecuted in the mid and far east.

General Eisenhower once challenged his staff about leadership using the example of a string. He laid out a string in a straight line and asked them to push it forward. The string went every which way. He pointed out that it is difficult to push a string but a string can be pulled by the example of leadership.

Hopefully, Christianity has progressed well beyond using the point of force and instead has become **the light that attracts people by their own free will** to come to Christ.

> • And I, if I be lifted up from the earth, will draw all men unto me. (John 12:32)

In summary, the kind of life that we lead as Christians will draw men to Christ, but we must lead by example and not force.

Attendee B: Thank you, Governor for sharing your insights.

Editor: Governor Smith, I'm the editor for the religion section of my newspaper and I'm here covering the prayer breakfast. The Declaration of Independence refers to **Nature's God** and *endowed by their **Creator** with certain unalienable Rights,* No doubt you support these phrases. However, the first amendment says that *Congress shall make no law respecting an establishment of religion, or prohibiting the free exercise thereof ...*

In Thomas Jefferson's correspondence, he referred to *a wall of separation between church and state.* While the "separation" phrasing is not in the Declaration of Independence or the Bill of Rights, it is widely believed that phrasing was the **intent** of the founders. Do you intend to honor that wall of separation?

RWS: When the constitution was written, there were numerous denominations. I think the founders, because of various denominational persecutions and conflicts in the past, did not want to enshrine any one of them as **the** state religion. These types of conflicts would divide a young nation. At the same time, they wanted to guarantee the free exercise of religion according to the **conscience** and wishes of citizens. I share these concepts.

You've heard the saying ***Don't throw out the baby with the bathwater.*** The founding fathers used the phrasing *Nature's God* and *endowed by their Creator.* You could argue the founding fathers intended a *wall of separation between **church** and state.* Do you think they intended *a wall of separation between **God** and state?*

Reporter: That does put it uniquely—God is pretty much a universal concept—understood by most of mankind. I think - I like your question.

6 BROTHES AND SISTERS
IN ADAM'S RACE

And Judah and Israel dwelled safely, every man under his vine and under his fig tree, from Dan even to Beersheba, all the days of Solomon. (I Kings 4:25)

Denver, Colorado, April 14, 2020

Governor R.W. Smith attended the International Multi-cultural Fair exhibit today and visited the exhibits of many nations and races from around the world—including the exhibit of the Cherokees from Oklahoma.

Since Governor's Smith's emergence from being a dark horse candidate to third place in the delegate count, he has been accompanied by a considerable flock of reporters. Afterward, he chatted at length with reporters in the rest hall between the Jamaican and Singapore exhibits. …

Reporter A: Governor Smith, what would a Smith Administration do to promote racial harmony? You are Christian in belief, but to some extent Christian churches tend to separate themselves into racial and economic strata.

RWS: There is a distinction between official government policy toward religion and my own personal beliefs. As you well know, the bill of rights gives us freedom to pursue our spiritual beliefs. Are you asking about this, or about my own religious beliefs?

Reporter A: I'm asking how your **personal** Christian beliefs would influence your **public** administration of government policies?

RWS: Let me put it this way, I do not believe that my Christian beliefs would cause a conflict with the duties of the president to uphold the constitution-- which is based on The Declaration of Independence.

Consider the harmony between these two statements:

> We hold these truths to be self-evident, that all men are created equal, that they are endowed by their Creator with certain unalienable Rights, that among these are Life, Liberty, and the pursuit of Happiness.

> - And has made of **one blood all nations of men** for to dwell on all the face of the earth, and has determined the times before appointed, and the bounds of their habitation;

- That they should seek the Lord, if haply they might feel after him, and find him, though he be not far from every one of us:
- For in him we live, and move, and have our being; as certain also of your own poets have said, **For we are also his offspring.**

  (Acts 17:26-28)

It seems to me that the wording in the Declaration of Independence may have sprung from the scripture in Acts. And in another place, the Apostle Paul said:

- **There is neither Jew nor Greek**, there is neither bond nor free, there is neither male nor female: for you are all one in Christ Jesus. (Galations 3:28).

I think that Martin Luther King got it right when he said that we should be judged by the content of our character, not by the color of our skin.

Reporter A: OK, I understand what you have said about race—but what about economic stratification which exists generally and to some extent in the churches? What about the poor?

RWS: Concerning the churches, I would say this; the poor should not be neglected or looked down upon because they are poor. The Apostle James gave this admonition:

- My brothers, have not the faith of our Lord Jesus Christ, the Lord of glory, with respect
- For if there come to your assembly a man with a gold ring, in goodly apparel, and there come in also a poor man in vile raiment;
- And you have respect to him that wears the gay clothing, and say to him, Sit you here in a good place; and say to the poor, Stand you there, or sit here under my footstool:
- **Are you not then partial in yourselves**, and are become judges of evil thoughts?

- Listen, my beloved brothers, **Has not God chosen the poor of this world** rich in faith, and heirs of the kingdom which he has promised to them that love him?
- **But you have despised the poor**. Do not rich men oppress you, and draw you before the judgment seats?
- Do not they blaspheme that worthy name by the which you are called?
- If you fulfill **the royal law** according to the scripture, **You shall love your neighbor as yourself**, you do well: (James 2:1-8)

Now, I will grant that for myself and for churches in general, that additional effort is needed to fulfill this admonition, but it is a worthy goal to be achieved.

Reporter B: Your answers touch on another point that has become very controversial—what should be the role of government in helping the poor? What about the inequalities between the rich and poor?

RWS: Jesus was confronted by the Pharisees about paying tribute to Caesar. His answer somewhat confounded them when he said, *Render therefore unto Caesar the things which are Caesar's; and unto God the things that are God's.*

So, basically, your question boils down to what is the division point between help to the poor by charities and help by the government? Charities are more efficient in supplying the point of need, but on the other hand government tries to insure that everyone's needs are met and no one is overlooked. Let's first look at this from a Christian perspective concerning the poor.

The Apostle Paul made trips and wrote letters to the churches in Corinth and Thessalonica in Greece. They were a part of the Roman Empire ruled by the Caesars at the time. These churches apparently had a charitable outreach much like churches of today help the poor.

Paul's described these activities in a similar way that modern day insurance pools function to even out peaks and valleys. Premiums of abundance cover losses in timc of need. You might even notice the buzzword 'equality' in this set of scriptures.

- **For if there be first a willing mind**, it is accepted according to that a man has, and not according to that he has not.
- For I mean **not that other men be eased, and you burdened:**
- But by an **equality**, that now at this time **your abundance** may be a supply for their want, that **their abundance** also may be a supply for your want: that there may be **equality**:
- As it is written, He that had gathered much had nothing over; and he that had gathered little had no lack. (II Corinthians 8:12-15)

Now, the above sounds very good and one might think that everyone lived happily ever after. But Paul also pointed out that problems with this system might arise. What did Paul mean when he said that there must *be first a willing mind*? Let's look at his admonishment about the administration of helping those in need.

- For even when we were with you, this we commanded you, that **if any would not work, neither should he eat.**
- For we hear that there are some which walk among you disorderly, **working not at all**, but are busybodies.
- Now them that are such we command and exhort by our Lord Jesus Christ, **that with quietness they work, and eat their own bread.** (2 Thessalonians 3:10-12)

Now, is Paul suggesting that the poor be starved—I don't think so. Instead, he is saying don't reward bad behavior. However, the scriptures do proscribe that assistance be given to the fatherless, widows and the sick and/or disabled.

Reporter B: What you say is quite interesting and you have outlined concepts that I didn't know were in the Bible. However, you boiled down the question to what is the division point in assistance to the poor between charities and the government, are you saying the government doesn't have a role in helping the poor?

RWS: Not at all, but the government needs to be quite careful that its actions do not aggravate the problems and cause them to grow worse. And secondly, charities tend to be much more efficient than government in helping the poor.

Reporter B: How so?

RWS: Let me relate to you a little down home story to illustrate my point—could be its not true, maybe it is and it's a good story.

It seems that one of our congressmen wanted to have his house painted before the winter, but he was leaving soon for Washington. A kid from down the road offered to do it, but he wasn't real bright. To counter this, the congressman purchased two five gallon buckets of paint and set them on the front porch. He then wrote out **very detailed instructions**

for painting and hoped for the best as he headed for the airport.

After several days, he phoned back to see how the kid was doing. He was pleased to learn the entire front of the house was painted and looked forward to a favorable completion schedule. A week later, he phoned back and found that only half of the north side had been completed. The congressman thought that more should have been done by then but got busy and it was three weeks later when he called back expecting that the painting had already been completed—but it wasn't—only half of the back of the house had been painted.

Frustrated, he called his brother to leave Oklahoma City and go up to the farm to check things out. After several hours, his brother called back and said the kid was still painting away but he had found the source of the slow progress problem.

The brother had asked the kid why it was taking so long. The kid said it went fast at first because the paint buckets were setting in front of the house. Then he said that it's a long way from the front of the house to the back and it takes time to run back and forth from the bucket to the back of the house to get a fresh dip of paint on the brush. The moral of the story is -

Reporter B: OK, OK, I don't think you need to elaborate on the point of the story – I get it.

RWS: Oh, I don't mind elaborating at all. The point is that the further management gets away from the activity, the more likely it is to get bureaucratized up and the funds gobbled up by unnecessary overhead! Better to let the local guys and gals handle it. It avoids all the top heavy, inefficient overhead. The feds would probably leave the paint buckets in the same position, hire another person to carry brushes dipped in fresh paint back and forth and then hire a supervisor to overlook the task—and maybe add a secretary to complete the paperwork and write CFR regulations for painting of all houses.

Perhaps you've heard of the term 'OPM'? It stands for Other People's Money. If those who dole out the money are in distant Washington, then those who receive the money no longer think of it as coming from their friends and neighbors. But, in the final analysis, it is fellow citizens that pay taxes.

Now, the question is—why is the federal government so inefficient? As you well know, in addition to the cabinet heads, the government has adopted the practice of appointing czars for this and that activities. Consider the story of Catherine the Great who decided on a whim to take a field trip down the river and through the Russian country side to see how the peasantry was getting along.

Her advisors were thrown into a tizzy because they had been giving her glowing reports of the excellent results of their administrative results. What if she got out of the palace and saw things as they really were?

Skilled in maintaining their bureaucracy, they came up with a scheme of mapping out a route in advance for her. But, there was so little time to make the improvements needed. **So, a plan was hatched to paint only the front of the houses that faced the river**; so that the empress would be impressed with the efficiency of her ministers. The palace ministers were determined to hold on to the cushy jobs.

Reporter B: Governor, from your stories and anecdotes, it is quite apparent that you think governmental overhead has become top heavy, intrusive, wasteful and very inefficient. But, let me go back to my earlier question: Where is the division point in helping the poor between government and charities?

RWS: One example would be the use of the military's capability in times of natural disaster to help in rescue and enable logistics of food supply and other basic needs. But, rather than trying to establish a division point, let's look at these efforts as a **partnership** between the government and charities—consider the work of the Red Cross, the Salvation Army and many similar charities.

Constructive Incentivization is a concept of structuring assistance programs so that those in need have incentives to make choices—choices that lift them out of dependency. So, someone falls off the bicycle and we provide training wheels. Does the assistance program reward them for keeping the training wheels rather than overcoming, if possible, and riding normally once again?

Something is very wrong when assistance programs create even more dependency rather than extraction from the initial need.

Reporter B: What makes you think that you will change anything when and **if** you get to the White House—we've heard all that before.

RWS: Yes, we certainly have. Will I be able to revise policies that reward bad behavior by creating more bad behavior?—I hope so. That is my plan.

Reporter B: Governor, you have been quoting scriptures to us—let me return the favor by quoting these scriptures to you.

- And all that believed were together, and had all things common;
- And sold their possessions and goods, and parted them to all men, as every man had need.
- And they, continuing daily with one accord in the temple, and breaking bread from house to house, did eat their meat with gladness and singleness of heart, (Acts 2:44-46)

Wouldn't you say these scriptures indicate a communal form of government?

RWS: It does for those who are in one accord and come together in free will for a common **spiritual** purpose. However, it seems your use of the word "government" is intended to apply to **secular government**—like that of a nation.

During dark centuries, learning was passed on through monasteries and convents which had singleness of spiritual purpose. Some transcribed scriptures into new copies of the Bible; some like St. Francis of Assisi's order helped the poor.

However, correct me if I'm wrong, but the thrust of your question seems to be toward having a secular government own everything and tell everyone what to do—voluntary or involuntary—it doesn't matter. Surrender unto Seizure the things that Caesar wants to seize; Render to the poor anything that's left over. The top dog sets the rules in a dog eat dog world.

I remember when I was twelve, my father's barn burned down during the winter, but fortunately he was a voluntary member of a farm co-op insurance plan. During good times, his premiums helped others—and he was then helped to restore the burned barn. In the meantime, our neighbors helped feed our farm animals.

One of the good ol' American institutions is a co-op to serve its members. It could be a farm co-op, a credit union, a carpool, or even a potluck church supper. Or, consider the pioneer days of the Christian camp meetings where people came from far and wide. The local Christians shared their food and facilities with visitors for the purpose of sharing the gospel.

This is in line with the theme of the very first church founded at Jerusalem hosting those that came for Pentecost from every nation to learn about Christ. They attended a college of intensive instruction in the gospel of Jesus Christ. Once the message was received through the Holy Spirit, they departed to evangelize their nation.

 But the key is a singleness of purpose and voluntary participation. Even in the church world, if some members of the Harmony Church disagree with other members, they can go down the road and build the New Harmony Church.

Audience: (Laughter)

Reporter C: Governor, there has been quite a bit of controversy in Colorado about the virtues of public education versus a voucher system allowing parents to choose private, religious or home schooling. I can probably guess where you stand on this, but in light of the recent controversy—would you please elaborate on your position.

RWS: No, need to elaborate. *Render therefore unto Caesar the things which are Caesar's; and unto God the things that are God's.* Do you have children?

Reporter C: Yes I do; a girl and a boy.

RWS: Children are a gift from God. So, what might your choice be? Are you pro-government or pro-family? Would you like for the state to mandate that choice for you and also the curricula that your child must study? Granted, free public education is an excellent way of insuring our children can learn the three R's and build upon that foundation. However, even in that area, in some cases, it is failing our children. Maybe a little competition through a voucher system would motivate public schooling to take a more critical inventory of its effectiveness.

I am reminded of the old farm story about the errant football flying over the fence into the chicken yard. The rooster gathered the hens around and said, "Ladies, mind you, I am not complaining, but look at what your competition is doing."

Audience: (Laughter)

Reporter C: Governor, I will not press you further on this; it is not difficult to figure out where your sympathies lie. You know, you have a curious habit of answering questions by asking questions.

RWS: Oh, I've been told that many times. I learned the technique from reading about Jesus in the Bible.

Governor's aide: Governor, our pilot says the sudden snow storm coming in over the Rockies may delay our departure. Suggest that we head out now and check status once we arrive at Rocky Mountain Metropolitan Airport.   …

7 UNDERDOG—GOLDEN RULE— OVERDOG

Salute every saint in Christ Jesus. The brethren which are with me greet you. All the saints salute you, chiefly they that are of Caesar's household. (Philippians 4:21-22)

Broomfield, Colorado, April 14, 2020

Governor R.W. Smith delayed his scheduled departure to the West coast due to the evening snow storm. An impromptu press conference was set up at the Hyatt which resulted in quite a dialog, both with reporters and some MURG (Multi-Umbrella Resource Group) protesters that got a whiff of the press conference and showed up to heckle the candidate. …

Reporter A: Governor, as you well know after attending the multi-cultural fair; many diverse ideas are presented by those manning the exhibits there—

ideas about social and moral issues. The battles have become fierce and heated at times. One side condemns the other's view points and vice versa— the condemnation rushes back the other way. As a president with Christian beliefs, what makes you think a Smith administration would rise above this?

RWS: The question you raise is a serious one and requires serious thought. Yes, there is an adversarial approach of an *eye for an eye and a tooth for a tooth.* However, in the musical *Fiddler on the Roof,* Tevye the dairyman observed that this would lead to a blind and toothless generation.

Reporter A: Governor, I think you have been quoted that science is just beginning to catch up with the truths in the Bible. Maybe social science isn't exactly what you meant—however, the eye and tooth verse is in the Bible—it was the law.

RWS: Did you graduate in law before becoming a reporter?

Reporter A: Yes, how did you know?

RWS: Oh, I just made a guess. Let me quote you a set of scriptures for lawyers:

- Then one of them, which was a lawyer, asked him a question, tempting him, and saying,
- Master, which is the great commandment in the law?

- Jesus said unto him, Thou shalt love the Lord thy God with all thy heart, and with all thy soul, and with all your mind.
- This is the first and great commandment.
- And the second is like unto it, **Thou shalt love thy neighbor as thyself.**
- **On these two commandments hang all the law** and the prophets. (Matthew 22:35-40)

The scriptures say that Jesus came to fulfill the law, not to destroy it. So, let me ask you a question: If you obey the two higher laws of love, would you break **any** of the ten commandments such as stealing or bearing false witness, etc?

Reporter A: No, I guess not—are you saying the law of love trumps the other laws?

RWS: True leadership requires getting past tit for tat condemnations of one another. It gets past the negative and accentuates positive alternatives. It is finding a way to love one another—a golden rule that is not only in the Bible but exists almost universally in cultures around the world.

Reporter A: Love is wonderful but as president, you will be enforcing laws and unfortunately there are still those who break laws.

RWS: Laws were embraced by the Hebrews through the ten commandments given by Moses. And later, Paul's ministry reached out to the Gentiles.

However, within mankind, **there are certain universal laws of conscience and nature.** The scriptures explain it this way.

- For when the **Gentiles, which have not the law, do by nature the things contained in the law,** these, having not the law, are a law unto themselves:
- Which show the **work of the law written in their hearts, their conscience also bearing witness,** and their thoughts the mean while accusing or else excusing one another;)

(Romans 2:14-15)

Whether stone tablets were brought down from the mountain—or not, mankind has been given a conscience and an understanding of actions which are in harmony with nature—or in disharmony with nature. It is not just Hebrews or Christians that hold these beliefs. This goes back **before** the time of the Hebrew Abraham or the birth of Jesus and Christianity into the world. It is the very conscience placed within mankind and cultures across the earth. There are those who rebel against their conscience and natural laws and try to drag others into their orbit because misery wants company.

Reporter A: What would be an example of disharmony with nature and going against one's conscience?

RWS: Probably one of the most egregious acts is

pedophilia. Even animals respect other animal's chastity until they have reached the age of puberty. **True love elevates the dignity of others rather than shames them.** Love is the golden rule and it is part of the inner conscience of mankind.

Reporter A: Well said, love is held in high esteem by philosophers, but still, from a Christian viewpoint, how do you deal with **the real world accusations** that clearly flow back and forth? They say that negative politics works—so isn't condemning your opponent just part of getting elected?

RWS: Let me put it this way: Most people are familiar with John 3:16 saying that *God so loved the world, that he gave his only begotten Son* ... But Christians must also remember the next verse:

- For God sent **not his Son into the world to condemn the world**; but that the world through him might be saved. (John 3:17)

Yes, the problem you have identified as back and forth condemnations is a challenge—a tough challenge. But true leadership leads by example and not by force.

MURG (Multi-Umbrella Resource Group): Governor Smith runs a hate campaign! Don't vote for him. The Bible has hate verses! Hate! Hate! Hate! Hate! Hate! Hate!

Security: Governor Smith, do you want us to remove the protesters from the conference room?

RWS: No, I will talk to them.

MURG: Don't vote for Smith! The Bible is a hate book! The Bible has hate verses! Hate! Hate! Hate!

RWS: What makes you think the Bible has hate verses—apparently, you disagree with what's in it?

Protester: We certainly do. Laws are needed to put it in its place—in the trash can!

RWS: Does your organization have books that teach your ideas? Do you have one with you?

Protester: So glad you asked! I'll give you one that tells what's wrong with the Bible.

RWS: I'll make you a deal. I have with me a small version of the Bible that contains the New Testament and the Psalms. I will give you my book and you can give me your book and we'll go outside and burn both books. How's that for a deal?

Protester: No, don't wanna do that.

RWS: Why not?

Protester: Well, maybe the fire code won't allow it.

RWS: Oh, there's lots of snow out there—shouldn't

be a problem. Isn't the real reason that you don't want me to burn your book is you don't want to be classified as a book burner? Why not let the ideas in the books compete with each other and let love and goodness triumph?

Protester: Burning the Bible would be bad PR for our cause—we don't have enough votes yet, but we will soon enough! You burn your own book—we're out of here!

Reporter B: Interesting exchange. OK, Governor Smith, you say you want to hold to a higher standard as a president and you just happen to be a Christian. But, realize that people and organizations exist that don't believe what you believe and find that while the New Testament teaches love; they find other parts of it offensive. How do you answer them?

RWS: Yes, I am quite acutely aware of that from my last campaign as governor. My path has been to be genuine in my beliefs and not try to hide my belief in the scriptures. God created each of us and loves each of us—and if he loves all mankind, we should too. Maybe Will Rogers captured this theme quite well when he said *I never met a man I didn't like.* The spirit of a human being is a gift from God.

Even among Christians, disagreements exist about how to interpret the scriptures, but to disregard their main thrust perhaps is to spiritually walk through a door with a sign over it reading **ENTER AT YOUR OWN RISK.**

On the other hand, an overly protective 'parent' government can stunt the growth of 'teenage' citizenry by trying to remove all risk.

When the apostles were the **underdog** under the Roman Empire masters, they were persecuted for their beliefs. They would have preferred that the emperor would have treated them according to the Golden Rule. Later, when Christians rose in power under recently converted Constantine there was an opportunity to practice the Golden Rule concerning those who did not accept the Christianity. Unfortunately, at various times under later 'Christian' emperors, tolerance disappeared and was replaced with persecution. The **underdog** became the **overdog**.

Trying to impose conversion upon unbelievers by force is not a conversion at all. In exchange for the right of Christians to believe according to their conscience, a tolerance must exist for beliefs of others. It is true that Christians expect that when Christ returns all nations will be drawn to him. But, in the meantime, Christians are admonished that they *are in the world but not of the world* and to *occupy till I come.*

Executive leaders of nations must realize that when people come for final judgment before the Most High, it is God who judges—not dictators, emperors, prime ministers, dear leaders, or presidents. A president can work to shape an environment of love, mercy and reconciliation, but final **spiritual** judgment of a person, be it vengeance or mercy, belongs to the Lord.

However, if certain groups do not agree with what is in the Bible, do you think it would be a good idea for them to burn someone else's Bible?

Reporter B: No, because as a reporter I do appreciate freedom of the press—even if I don't agree with all that is written in any given book, or even ancient ones. You know, Governor Smith, I've been listening to all this idea of love trumping everything, and it strikes me as being 'pie in the sky'. A president has to deal with tough situations and sometimes make agonizing decisions—what about the real world of dog eat dog?

RWS: What you say about tough situations is quite true. My model of how to handle adversity comes from what I learned from my sophomore year summer job foreman. We worked in a shop that repaired bulldozers.

This foreman was the embodiment of Solomon's proverb that *A soft answer turns away wrath.* But, the secretary who worked there told me, "Don't let that fool you; they call him the Velvet Bulldozer. If you're not straight with him, you will experience the motivational steel dozer blade under the soft velvet and the piercing gaze of tough, but kind, eyes."

8 EXPANDING OUR VISION

Pasadena, CA, May 26, 2020

With only a week to go before the make or break California primary, Governor R.W. Smith held a huge and enthusiastic rally at the Pasadena Convention Center. Earlier in the day he had visited the Jet Propulsion Laboratory and the Mt. Wilson Observatory where Edwin Hubble made his breakthrough discoveries. After the rally, Governor Smith met with reporters, a number of which represented scientific blogs and journals.

…

From this newspaper writer's experience in covering political campaigns, it seems quite unusual for a presidential candidate to be involved in detailed discussions about science and the Bible. However, since Governor Smith's views have shown up in a negative way in a few campaign ads, inevitably detailed questions will be posed by science journalists.

...

Journalist A: Governor Smith, your oft-replayed video statement "Science is only now beginning to catch up with the truths revealed in the Bible." is causing some controversy among scientists and even ridicule by parts of the media. In retrospect, do you wish that you had not made that statement?

RWS: No.

Journalist A: I see. As you know, you are standing in the midst of technological giants such as NASA's Jet Propulsion Laboratory, Cal-Tech and the Mt. Wilson observatory. So, in the very shadow of all this modern technology, would you care to defend your statement?

RWS: Glad to do so. I was told at the observatory that many of Hubble's significant discoveries were made in the 1920's—such as multiple galaxies and the red-shift effect resulting from an expansion of the universe. And his discoveries are deservedly applauded.

But is this information really new or is it something that described in ancient scripture? First, let's consider Hubble's astonishment when he discovered what had been thought to be stars were actually galaxies comparable to our own Milky Way. The number of stars and galaxies he discovered was beyond his ability to number. Is this that much different than the Bible's metaphor of an exponential and projected and ever-continuing growth of Abraham's seed?

- Therefore sprang there even of one, and him as good as dead, so many **as the stars of the sky in multitude**, and as the sand which is by the sea shore **innumerable** _(Hebrews 11:12)

Journalist A: Oh, come on, the ancients knew a lot of stars existed in the sky, what else?

RWS: OK, perhaps you know that the giants of physics, Albert Einstein and Fred Hoyle resisted Edwin Hubble's expansion proposals. However, let's look at some of the expansion statements from the Bible. Would you admit that the words expanding and stretching out are similar?

Journalist A: Yes, that seems reasonable.

RWS: Consider these verses from the Bible:

- He **stretches out** the north over the empty place, and **hangs the earth on nothing**.
  (Job 26:7)

- Bless the LORD, O my soul. O LORD my God, you are very great; you are clothed with honor and majesty.
- Who cover yourself with light as with a garment: **who stretch out the heavens like a curtain:** (Psalms 104:1-2)

- Have you not known? have you not heard? has it not been told you from the beginning? have

64

you not understood from the foundations of the earth?

- It is he that sits on **the circle of the earth**, and the inhabitants thereof are as grasshoppers; that **stretches out the heavens as a curtain, and spreads them out as a tent to dwell in:** (Isaiah 40:21-22)

Since you write for a prestigious scientific journal, I'm sure that you are aware of studies[10] that refer to the term *fabric of the cosmos*—are you not?

Journalist A: Yes, it is commonly described that way.

RWS: Good. Now, consider the wording in the last two sets of verses from the Psalms and from Isaiah. Would you not agree *that stretch out the heavens like a curtain* **and** *stretches out the heavens as a curtain and spreads them out as a tent to dwell in* is similar to the description of a fabric?

Journalist A: Well, maybe—somewhat similar.

RWS: OK, here's a question for you. Edwin Hubble's work revealed that the number of stars could be in the billions, trillions, or who knows how great a number. Look at this image of Milky Way, I'm holding up on my tablet. I have been told that astronomers have estimated that up to four hundred billion stars exist in the Milky Way alone.[11]

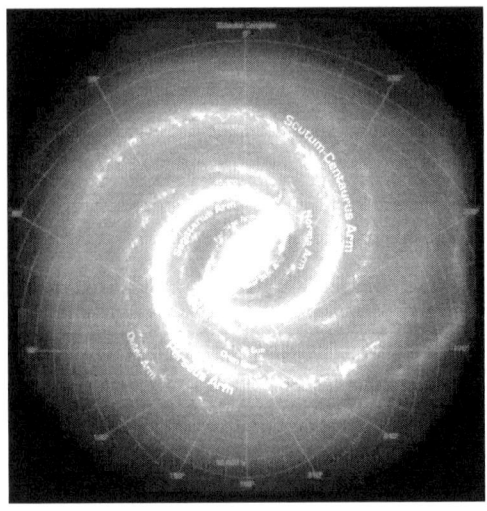

Milky Way, Image credit, NASA

Given, the huge, huge number of stars and galaxies do you think a high probability exists that an intelligent civilization somewhat like earth exists somewhere out there—or even possibly closer to home in our own Milky way?

Journalist A: Well, since intelligent civilization exists here on earth, it seems probable with the huge number of possibilities that it is likely to exist elsewhere. Maybe—considering all the wars on this earth—they hopefully would be even more intelligent than we are.

RWS: If a more intelligent civilization exists, somewhere, do you think **its leader might be God?**

Journalist A: Uh, I hadn't thought of it that way –

Journalist B: Governor, Smith, we are supposed to be interviewing you, not you questioning us. Now, instead of answering our questions with a question, please give an example of how you think science is just now beginning to catch up with the Bible.

RWS: OK, I think that you would agree that the universities in California are on the cutting edge of scientific discovery. One of the theories that began developing in the 1970's was that matter was composed of vibrating strings. And then, in the 1990's the concept that these strings were attached to a stretchable membrane was added. Now a stretchable membrane or fabric is similar to this wording: *stretches out the heavens as a curtain, and spreads them out as a tent to dwell in.*

Now, it seems that string and membrane theorists have strangely enough come to propose that hidden dimensions exist. Now, while you are familiar with this theory, I see a blank look on some of the people here. So, permit me to elaborate just a bit.

See the clock on the wall. It now reads four hours, 59 minutes and 50 seconds. Now, let's pause just a bit … Now, it reads five hours, 0 minutes and 5 seconds. It is obvious that this clock has space dimensions of length, width and depth. Since, we looked at the clock at one time and then we looked at it 15 seconds later, it has a dimension of time. These are what scientists call the four 'seen' dimensions of our everyday life and familiarity.

Now, it seems that in addition to the **four 'seen' dimensions**, scientists are now saying that **seven 'hidden' dimensions** exist. Would you please explain for the group your knowledge of what lies hidden in these hidden dimensions? ...

Oh, sorry, I'm not supposed to be asking you questions. However, given the present state of knowledge, it seems unlikely that anyone has yet explained to any degree what is invisible to us. However, the Bible does have something to say about the relationship between the visible and the invisible.

- Through faith we understand that the worlds were framed by the word of God, **so that things which are seen were not made of things which do appear.** (Hebrews 11:3)

Now, curiously, the Bible does describe the **Seven Spirits of God** and a rainbow around the throne in the fourth chapter of Revelation. Since it's getting late, I won't go there, but you can check it out. Seven Spirits = seven hidden dimensions?

How do you describe something that's invisible and not much is known about? My solution to this problem is to use a metaphor.

Suppose you are sitting in a totally dark room which has only a little pinhole as a window. You entered the room at midnight and stumbled through the darkness to sit on a stool. You can sense the dimensions of length, width and depth of the stool (three dimensions) and you have a sense of the passage of time making four dimensions.

Then you hear a rooster crow and soon after—a small beam of light pierces the darkness through the pinhole. You sense a new dimension entering the room. But wait, is it just one dimension or is it more? You take a glass prism out of your pocket and hold it in the light beam. Then it 'dawns upon you' that what you thought was one dimension is actually the seven colors of the rainbow. And I would like to add scripture here about our partial comprehension as we gaze through the glass.

- **For now we see through a glass, darkly**; but then face to face: now I know in part; but then shall I know even as also I am known.
- And now stays faith, hope, charity, these three; but the greatest of these is charity. (I Corinthians 13:12-13)

So, my scientific journalist friend, I have given you an example, and if I may be permitted to ask a question, does this suffice as an example?

Journalist B: Interesting example, as you point out, you used a metaphor—however, I'm not sure that our present day scientists really understand the hidden dimensions either. They just know that the mathematics works if they use four space-time dimensions and seven hidden dimensions. But, let me do a follow-up question—what is your position on the intelligent design vs: evolution debate?

RWS: Oh, I'm all for evolution—mini-evolution within a given species. However, a significant number of scientists are having problems with the classic Darwin model. The very complexity of the design of the human body says that intelligent design was required.

Consider that there are about 100 trillion cells[12] in the human body and within each cell is the DNA library. Then, imagine taking some tiny tweezers and trying to poke the information of multiple, multiple, encyclopedias into **each** of 100 trillion cells.

Gee, Watson and Crick received the Nobel Prize for their DNA discoveries in 1962 and scientists are still scratching their head trying to understand it for fifty plus years.

Scientists have been somewhat successful in modifying DNA, but one thing has been consistently missing—**initiation** of life itself. They have to hijack an existing life form for a starting point for their modifications. Modification, yes; creation, no — perhaps creation does require a Creator and the designs are written in the manufacturer's instruction handbook.

- I will praise you; for **I am fearfully and wonderfully made:** marvelous are your works; and that my soul knows right well.
- My substance was not hid from you, when I was made in secret, and curiously worked in the lowest parts of the earth.

70

- Your eyes did see my substance, yet being imperfect; and **in your book all my members were written, which in continuance were fashioned, when as yet there was none of them.** (Psalms 139:14-16)

Could we at least grudgingly admit there may have been just a tad of intelligent design behind the DNA model? Oh, I shouldn't have asked a question, but understand that it was a rhetorical one.

Foreign Press Reporter A: Let me change the subject a bit. Previous questions have centered on science and your Christian beliefs. Didn't Jesus say if someone smites you on the right cheek turn the other cheek to him also? How would a President Smith handle a slap on this nation's cheek by a hostile nation?

RWS: There is a proverb that a *false balance is abomination to the LORD: but a just weight is his delight.* Finding that balance applies to more than just goods and money—it also applies to our responses. Yes, it is true that Jesus was meek and walked in a lamb-like nature, but also isn't it true that he showed the Lion of Judah nature when he turned over the tables of the corrupt money changers in the temple? A Smith administration would seek a **proper balance** in responding to hostility and perhaps might even turn over the tables of those involved in corruption. One last question and then I must leave to attend a banquet.

Network reporter A: The polls still show you as the underdog in the California primary. Maybe the party candidate will be finally selected in an open convention. Do you think you can pull off an upset and win the race?

RWS: Hopefully, I will win, God willing. However, whether my fate is to win or lose, I have a personally more important race to run and that is *to press toward the mark for the prize of the high calling of God in Christ Jesus.* My destiny is in the hands of the most High God.

God Bless.

9 ADDITIONAL RESOURCES

Those running for political office well know the pitfalls of comments made during interviews and/or debates. The biblical admonition to be *wise as serpents, and harmless as doves* certainly applies.

Candidates are public figures and as such soon learn their words are subject to intense scrutiny. One misstep can generate what reporters love to call a firestorm of criticism—better to bridle the tongue than to try to stuff the toothpaste back into the tube.

- Behold, we put bits in the horses' mouths, that they may obey us; and we turn about their whole body.
- Behold also the ships, which though they be so great, and are driven of fierce winds, yet are they turned about with a very small helm, wherever the governor wants.

- Even so **the tongue is a little member, and boasts great things**. Behold, how great a matter a little fire kindles! (James 3:3-5)

Jesus walked this earth with the meekness of a lamb, but at times, he roared with the boldness of the Lion of Judah. Candidates need to seek that proper balance as the situation at hand merits.

If a Christian politician decides to venture into the arena of discussions of interactions between current scientific knowledge and the Bible it is best to be well prepared. This book presents only a few brief highlights of subjects that may arise in a campaign.

There are many, many other examples that could have been discussed such as the intertwining of the seven lamped Hebrew candle stick with hidden dimensions, anatomy, genetics, language and mathematics.

Another example is the lesson that can be learned from observing the chaos and darkness of the swaddling cloth of the earth's twin planet Venus—where amazingly for us tradition-bound earthlings—the time for the planet's **one year orbit around the sun is shorter** than the time the planet takes to complete a **day's rotation on its axis.**

- When I made the cloud the garment thereof, and thick darkness a swaddling cloth for it,

(Job 38:9)

Can a year be shorter than a day?

What might be done to lighten the intense, cloud shrouded darkness on Venus so the familiar sun appears during the daytime and the stars *rule the night* sky? Would changing Venus' 3 degree axial tilt[13] to near the 23.5 degree axial tilt of the earth give it proper orientation *for signs, and for seasons?* What about increasing Venus' axial rotation rate to give it proper *days, and years*?

- And the earth was without form, and void; and darkness was on the face of the deep. And the Spirit of God moved on the face of the waters.
- And God said, Let there be light: and there was light. (Genesis 1:2-3)

It is wisdom to be well briefed and to have a deeper understanding of the subject matter when giving an interview or campaigning. Those seeking additional information should follow-up by reading the book *Waters of Creativity*. This book presents twelve presidential style no-holds barred debates between participants ranging from atheist and/or secular scientists to Christians with scientific credentials.

Many of the topics in this book *So ~ You're a Christian Politician* were directly adopted from the *Waters of Creativity* book.

See   http://WatersofCreativity.com/

CHAPTER NOTES

The citations given are referenced with the understanding that their use in this book does not necessarily imply the source's agreement or disagreement with the themes of *So ~ You're a Christian Politician?*

PREFACE

1

COVER PHOTO
http://en.wikipedia.org/wiki/File:Broadcaster_Don_
Durbridge.png (Accessed 1/1/2014)

2

Waters of Creativity book by Mortimer J. Duck and Emily L. Duck (2013) Available through Amazon, Barnes and Noble, Books a Million, Christian Book Distributors, and other outlets. http://WatersofCreativity.com

3

http://www.angelfire.com/al4/allenkc/akjv/
Michael Peter (Stone) Engelbrite
Author of American King James Version
(Accessed 1/1/2014)

CHAPTER 1

4

These are comments made by Apollo 12 Astronaut Alan Bean in a 2012 Science Channel presentation entitled *NASA's Unexplained Files*. This flight followed Neil Armstrong and Buzz Aldrin's moon landing.

CHAPTER 3

5

http://en.wikipedia.org/wiki/Discovery_of_cosmic_microwave_ba
ckground_radiation (Accessed 1/1/2014)

6

http://en.wikipedia.org/wiki/File:Ilc_9yr_moll4096.png
(Accessed 1/1/2014)

7

http://en.wikipedia.org/wiki/Princeton_University
(Accessed 1/1/2014)

8

http://en.wikipedia.org/wiki/File:Magnetosphere_rendition.jpg
(Accessed 1/1/2014)

CHAPTER 8

9

http://en.wikipedia.org/wiki/File:Jetstreamconfig.jpg
from the U.S. National Oceanic and Atmospheric Administration
(Accessed 1/1/2014)

10

Book by Columbia University Physicist Brian Greene entitled *The Fabric of the Cosmos*
http://en.wikipedia.org/wiki/Brian_Greene   (Accessed 1/1/2014)

11

 http://www.universetoday.com/102630/ How Many Stars are There in the Universe?, Fraser Cain, (Accessed 1/1/2014)

12

http://en.wikipedia.org/wiki/Cell_(biology)
(Accessed 1/1/2014)

13

http://www.nasa.gov/audience/foreducators/postsecondary/features/F_Planet_Seasons.html (Accessed 1/5/2014)

So ~ You're a Christian Politician?